# Cancer
## ... and I

# Cancer ... and I

**A 365 Day Guided Diary to Journal Your Cancer Emotions**

## Ronell Grobler

First Edition: 2015
ISBN 10: 1518619193
ISBN 13: 9781518619199
Published by: Amazon
Printed in: USA/Europe
Cover design by: CreateSpace
Interior design by: CreateSpace

# ABOUT THE AUTHOR

I am Ronell Grobler, a qualified therapist. I am also an expatriate and have lived in the Middle East with my family for more than seven years.

No, I do not have cancer. I have seen cancer up close and personal, but I have never been in your shoes and will not for one moment think that I know what it is like.

I did, however, grow up in a family where my father, mother, and brother all had different types of cancer, which they had to deal with over extended periods of time. Recently another family member and my dearest friend dealt with cancer as well. In my professional life, I've also had the opportunity to work with people who have been affected by traumatic events and had to facilitate their support and recovery.

So, cancer and trauma have been on my mind a lot over the years. I've researched it, I've read about it extensively, and I've had numerous conversations with cancer survivors. I am no expert on cancer; I have just been around it almost all of my life and have witnessed, firsthand, the effect it has on people.

It is from this perspective that I have felt the need to provide a tool to serve people who are confronted with a cancer diagnosis. More often than not, the psyche is neglected when

v

the focus is on healing the physical; we have to heal our minds as well.

If this diary can help one person through his or her journey, then I've attained my goal to relieve suffering. I hope and wish that it may serve you in some small way to get through what you're facing.

# CONTENTS

# ACKNOWLEDGMENTS

*I* want to thank my wonderful husband and children, who unconditionally support me in everything I do. You give me purpose. Thanks also to my dearest friend, who inspired me.

# INTRODUCTION

## What This Diary Is All About

This diary is structured to include the stages that many people go through when confronted with trauma, such as being diagnosed with cancer.

There are three different prompts per day to help guide you through 365 days of dealing with your cancer. The diary spreads over a year, as this is the basic time frame by which we order our lives. You can start with the diary on the day of or shortly after your diagnosis, which should generally be your day 1 of 365. However, it is perfectly OK to start at a stage that you deem yourself to be in at the time of getting hold of the diary. It is designed in such a way that you may move back and forth—not like your normal diary!

The diary should be a practical guide to living with a cancer diagnosis. It is meant to provide structure to the enormous number of random thoughts and emotions you will experience as you progress. Although the diary is structured to flow chronologically, it might not correspond in all aspects to your process. As mentioned, you should feel free to move back and forth in the book as you wish and deem appropriate at the time.

This diary is not a self-help guide. It is only meant to help you record your deeply personal journey with cancer. It is a tool for recording those feelings that sometimes get left behind in the extensive (and bewildering) medical processes you might be facing and enduring. It can serve as a reliable point of reference for the psychological side of what you're going through as you continue along this path.

You should feel free to answer, comment, or embellish as you wish. The prompts are meant to stimulate your thoughts, and you can answer as you see fit, whether that be with a single word or a detailed description. Use descriptions, examples, references, or any manner that can express how you feel. Use the diary to reflect on yourself, get it all out, and clean your head and heart. Tap into your deepest emotions, and be honest. Try to record your emotions daily, for you will not remember all of them.

If a specific prompt does not pertain to you, try to imagine how you would have felt or what you would have done in that situation.

You can take what help you need from this diary. You can use it as a reminder with a therapist or in a support group. It can be used, at your discretion, to share with a loved one when you find it hard to communicate. From time to time, you can look back at what you've written to gain some insight into your emotions. Reflecting on your answers should help you see your emotional progress.

Upon completion of the diary, you should be able to look back on a year in which you've grown emotionally. You'll see that your capacity to deal with trauma in a more structured way has increased, and you'll realize there might be positive elements to what you've had to endure and that you are stronger for it!

# DAYS 1–31
# SHOCK AND DENIAL

Cancer happens to people, and now it has happened to you. Being diagnosed with cancer is an immense shock to anyone, and the emotions that accompany such news are normal and to be expected. Being sad and angry is OK. Wanting to deny that you have cancer is a way that your mind is attempting to handle the initial shock. Denial is one way of attempting to cope with news that seems, initially, too hard to handle. In order to deal with some of these emotions, one has to recognize them as they arise. One way to do that is to write them down. To bottle up such feelings can lead to psychological distress, which is not helpful to the medical process that you will be undergoing as a result of your cancer. Sitting down and putting associated fears and feelings on paper will provide you with a bit of quiet time, and every word you put down shall be a tiny step in moving forward. People cope with emotional distress in different ways. There is no right or wrong way to do this; however, by voicing the turmoil of emotions on paper, you will, over time, become increasingly aware as to how the diagnosis has been affecting you emotionally. This is all part of dealing and coping on an emotional level.

I was told that I have...

_____

_____

_____

When I heard I had cancer, I...

_____

_____

_____

The fear that went through me felt like...

_____

_____

_____

I need time to digest...

_____

_____

_____

Why me?

_____

_____

_____

What will happen to my body?

_____

_____

_____

My reaction to the diagnosis was...

_____

_____

_____

I was numbed with disbelief when...

_____

_____

_____

Cancer is the beginning of...

_____

_____

_____

Being diagnosed with cancer feels like...

_____

_____

_____

My treatment options are...

_____

_____

_____

I broke down when...

_____

_____

_____

Will I ever...

_____

_____

_____

I want to close my eyes and...

_____

_____

_____

It feels so unfair that...

_____

_____

_____

I am saddest about...

_____

_____

_____

My dominant thought before I go to sleep is...

_____

_____

_____

My first thought today was...

_____

_____

_____

Once the initial shock has subsided, I...

_____

_____

_____

This flood of emotions feels like...

_____

_____

_____

I want to survive cancer because...

_____

_____

_____

How much will all this cost?

_____

_____

_____

The financial implications of my cancer are...

_____

_____

_____

Concerns I have about money include...

_____

_____

_____

I want to withdraw from...

_____

_____

_____

It is so frightening to...

_____

_____

_____

The one question I ask myself is...

_____

_____

_____

Date:......................

The scary thing about cancer is...

_____

_____

_____

Making complex decisions at this stressful time can
feel like...

_____

_____

_____

The fine line between calm and panic is...

_____

_____

_____

What will happen if I cannot cope?

_____

_____

_____

I am still confused about...

_____

_____

_____

Sometimes I try to deny...

_____

_____

_____

I am terrified of...

_____

_____

_____

I am struggling with...

_____

_____

_____

A way to talk back to negativity is...

_____

_____

_____

I am most scared of...

I am overwhelmed by...

It is natural to feel lonely after a cancer diagnosis...

How do I confront my cancer?

_____

_____

_____

I try to discuss my concerns with...

_____

_____

_____

Now that I have cancer, I must first...

_____

_____

_____

Sleep...

_____

_____

_____

Food...

_____

_____

_____

People around me...

_____

_____

_____

How exactly did this happen?

_____

_____

_____

The question I ask the most is...

_____

_____

_____

I tell people...

_____

_____

_____

Cancer can...

_____

_____

_____

Cancer cannot...

_____

_____

_____

I don't have to face cancer alone because...

_____

_____

_____

Feelings of sadness, fear, and worry are natural...

_____

_____

_____

I must not judge myself for my emotions, especially...

_____

_____

_____

I try to encourage myself to...

_____

_____

_____

How will my family cope?

_____

_____

_____

How can I deal with the emotions and beliefs of my family?

_____

_____

_____

Who is going to care for my family's emotions through this?

_____

_____

_____

I can find strength in sharing thoughts and feelings with...

_____

_____

_____

Communication with my health-care team includes...

_____

_____

_____

Today I will try to...

_____

_____

_____

Being labeled as a person with cancer feels...

_____

_____

_____

It is hard to think about anything but my diagnosis, especially when...

_____

_____

_____

It feels like my cancer is uprooting everything, especially...

_____

_____

_____

There is nothing fair about cancer, and nobody deserves it...

_____

_____

_____

I have to try not to shut down mentally when...

_____

_____

_____

Facing the demands that come with cancer is...

_____

_____

_____

I am still trying to figure out what this cancer means to me, especially...

_____

_____

_____

Is cancer a roadblock to a life full of happiness?

_____

_____

_____

How can thinking positive thoughts help me over-come this roadblock?

_____

_____

_____

I cannot allow cancer to change my sense of self...

_____

_____

_____

Letting go of some old beliefs might help me cope with new ones...

_____

_____

_____

It is hard to understand why this is happening to me now...

_____

_____

_____

What can I do to make it better?

_____

_____

_____

Will I be healthy again?

_____

_____

_____

The best thing in my life right now is...

_____

_____

_____

What does my life mean right now?

_____

_____

_____

My cancer is real...

_____

_____

_____

Taking things one step at a time means...

_____

_____

_____

Having respect for life is...

_____

_____

_____

The losses and changes that cancer might bring include...

_____

_____

_____

It is sometimes hard to vent my feelings in a constructive way...

_____

_____

_____

I will never regret...

_____

_____

_____

Being alive has taken on a new dimension...

_____

_____

_____

Many of my emotions seem more intense, such as...

_____

_____

_____

I love my...

_____

_____

_____

The people in my life...

_____

_____

_____

Happiness is...

_____

_____

_____

Whatever way I choose to deal with this, I...

_____

_____

_____

Taking charge of my situation means...

_____

_____

_____

I don't have to be composed all the time, especially
when...

_____

_____

_____

Cancer is really happening to me, so I...

_____

_____

_____

I don't have to pretend that...

_____

_____

_____

Moving forward now means...

_____

_____

_____

DAYS 32–61

MY PROCESS

The uncertainties associated with your process will result in fear. This is also normal and to be expected. Your process is a very personal one. Use the pages of this diary as a tool to record and identify what feelings you are dealing with every day. Take the time to think it through so that you'll be able to reflect and have some degree of control over what you are experiencing on a deeply emotional level. By writing down your feelings, you should gradually be able to start identifying feelings that serve to elevate your mood, considering your circumstances, so that you can move forward with coming to grips with it all. Every cancer experience is unique and very personal (i.e., it cannot be described in terms of a series of events that one can study and understand in order to be appropriately prepared), and yours will be no different. You're the one who should know your intimate feelings best and how intense they are. If you do not record them, you will probably struggle to recall all your thoughts on this. Reflecting on the record of your feelings in the pages of this diary regularly will assist you to identify when you've been strong in your resolve and when you've been in need of some guidance or support. It will provide you with a sense of independence (i.e., not to be at the mercy of all the people around you). This in itself will help you feel as though you're strong in dealing with your experience.

I don't want to limit the things I enjoy just because I have cancer, especially...

_____

_____

_____

An immediate way to deal with this challenge might be...

_____

_____

_____

Treatment is a process, and that means...

_____

_____

_____

I am curious about...

_____

_____

_____

I am honest about...

_____

_____

_____

Uncertainty about exactly how the process will unfold makes me...

_____

_____

_____

How will my cancer affect my work situation?

_____

_____

_____

Will I be able to function at the same level at work?

_____

_____

_____

How active can I be each day?

_____

_____

_____

Understanding the extent of what is happening is...

_____

_____

_____

I need encouragement to...

_____

_____

_____

Still living my life fully means...

_____

_____

_____

It is easy for me to depend on...

_____

_____

_____

A way to soothe my spirit during this journey is...

_____

_____

_____

At this moment, the obstacles to my happiness are...

_____

_____

_____

For support, I need to turn to...

_____

_____

_____

Connecting with a cancer support group is...

_____

_____

_____

Cancer education is...

_____

_____

_____

Waking up with cancer every morning feels...

_____

_____

_____

I can guard against emotional distress by...

_____

_____

_____

I can actively participate in my treatment process by...

_____

_____

_____

Discussing treatment with my doctor is...

_____

_____

_____

I gather more information on cancer by...

_____

_____

_____

I need to focus on wellness because...

_____

_____

_____

If I look at my situation positively, how is it different?

_____

_____

_____

My family's combined strengths will...

_____

_____

_____

What can I do to enjoy meaningful days?

_____

_____

_____

Should I just focus on my cancer at the moment?

_____

_____

_____

My emotional go-to people are...

_____

_____

_____

A way to broaden my social support is...

_____

_____

_____

How can I integrate my cancer with my life?

Is my cancer just a disease, or is it me?

My chances of living through cancer are...

What I understand least about the cancer process is...

_____

_____

_____

I still need some clarification on...

_____

_____

_____

What will enable me to expand my perspective now?

_____

_____

_____

I want to nurture my inner strengths because...

_____

_____

_____

Setting realistic goals amid cancer is...

_____

_____

_____

Can other cancer survivors help me in any way?

_____

_____

_____

Fighting cancer requires me to...

_____

_____

_____

To monitor my mental processes, I...

_____

_____

_____

To cultivate a healthy mind, I...

_____

_____

_____

The strain on my physical and emotional energy is...

Is it a myth that a positive attitude can help heal my cancer?

Handling my day-to-day responsibilities requires...

Cancer education helps to...

_____

_____

_____

My mental coping strategy involves...

_____

_____

_____

Looking ahead, I feel...

_____

_____

_____

Relaxation...

_____

_____

_____

Exercise...

_____

_____

_____

Music...

_____

_____

_____

I am happy to...

_____

_____

_____

Something I did well today was...

_____

_____

_____

A motivating message to myself...

_____

_____

_____

I want to talk about cancer because...

_____

_____

_____

I have to be strong for...

_____

_____

_____

It is possible to...

_____

_____

_____

I don't want to talk about my cancer all the time because...

_____

_____

_____

I am allowed to take time away from...

_____

_____

_____

A thoughtful manner can prevent emotions from building up and...

_____

_____

_____

Date:...........................

A constructive coping mechanism for me is...

_____

_____

_____

Today is another day to...

_____

_____

_____

Does talking about cancer humanize the disease?

_____

_____

_____

A persistent empty mood is unhealthy because...

_____

_____

_____

I manage emotional distress by...

_____

_____

_____

Sleep disturbances are...

_____

_____

_____

I need to hear uplifting stories about...

_____

_____

_____

The stress-relieving activities that work well for me are...

_____

_____

_____

Striving for a cheery disposition might...

_____

_____

_____

It has already been fifty-five days, and...

_____

_____

_____

Being alive means...

_____

_____

_____

Realistic expectations about my cancer are...

_____

_____

_____

How do I take care of my family's feelings?

_____

_____

_____

Looking back on the past month, I...

_____

_____

_____

Positive self-talk can help me to...

_____

_____

_____

The external resources I rely on are...

_____

_____

_____

Joining a support group is...

_____

_____

_____

Sharing with other cancer patients...

_____

_____

_____

If I don't want to be pressured to be blindly positive, I have to...

_____

_____

_____

Optimism during cancer should not exclude sadness, anger, or...

_____

_____

_____

Through this difficult process, I will try to move
forward in life by...

_____

_____

_____

I now have to fulfil multiple roles: the cancer patient and the...

_____

_____

_____

I've done a good job of...

_____

_____

_____

Going down this road is...

_____

_____

_____

Date:..........................

Some relationships have deepened, such as...

_____

_____

_____

Being here for my family for a long time to come will mean...

_____

_____

_____

Meaningful outcomes of my cancer would be...

_____

_____

_____

Up until now, the biggest change I have undergone
is...

_____

_____

_____

The support community is...

_____

_____

_____

Things facilitating my process are...

_____

_____

_____

# DAYS 62–92

# MY BODY AND MY TREATMENTS

The dreaded "C" word is now part of your everyday life. Thinking about your body is an automatic response, especially after a treatment. Sometimes you might not like your body as much, and other times you might be more gracious in these thoughts. Is it not better to give your body the benefit of the doubt, to believe that it might be otherwise strong on a path to healing? Although the treatments hurt and make you feel sick, they have to happen in order for you to become physically better again. Recognize when you become anxious and come up with ways to diminish that. Thinking and expecting the worst won't take the effects away; however, a deep and intimate knowledge of your experience on an emotional level will, over time, teach you through experience and reflection how to cope and hang on when again encountering similar emotions. So do that. Write these emotions down, read them again, digest them, and grow from there as a result.

Treatment changes the way a body looks, works, and feels:

_____

_____

_____

The visible effects of my treatment are...

_____

_____

_____

I contribute to my medical process by...

_____

_____

_____

Some effects of treatment can be temporary but
still upsetting, such as...

_____

_____

_____

The sooner I confront physical changes, the easier
I might...

_____

_____

_____

The initial intense feeling I have now is...

_____

_____

_____

I manage the physical changes in my body by...

_____

_____

_____

Sometimes I feel that my body has let me down,
especially when...

_____

_____

_____

Mortality is...

_____

_____

_____

To accept the changes in my body, I have to...

_____

_____

_____

Should I compare my treatment-related symptoms
with others'?

_____

_____

_____

All my body's aches and pains...

_____

_____

_____

The process so far...

_____

_____

_____

My prognosis so far is...

_____

_____

_____

Is it OK to think about my own frailty?

_____

_____

_____

Sleep brings...

_____

_____

_____

My appetite is...

_____

_____

_____

Intimacy feels...

_____

_____

_____

I sometimes feel awkward and uncomfortable when...

_____

_____

_____

The more I look at and feel my body, the less different it will seem; therefore...

_____

_____

_____

The uncertainty of how my body will react to treatment is...

_____

_____

_____

Pampering myself is important because...

_____

_____

_____

Alternative ways to manage my pain and feelings
are...

_____

_____

_____

Mood swings are...

_____

_____

_____

Experiencing a loss of confidence in my body feels...

_____

_____

_____

Changes to my body image from the cancer and treatment include...

_____

_____

_____

I feel weak and vulnerable while others are in good health...

_____

_____

_____

Before treatment days, I...

_____

_____

_____


Having pain affects my thoughts and feelings...

_____

_____

_____


I feel outside of my body when...

_____

_____

_____

I find it hardest to deal with...

_____

_____

_____

The aftereffects of a treatment include...

_____

_____

_____

The most practical way to deal with aftereffects is...

_____

_____

_____

During a treatment, I...

_____

_____

_____

My primary caregivers help me to...

_____

_____

_____

How will I heal?

_____

_____

_____

Feeling tired...

_____

_____

_____

Feeling sick...

_____

_____

_____

Nighttime...

_____

_____

_____

I try to appreciate my body's resilience by...

_____

_____

_____

The pressure of surviving cancer can be...

_____

_____

_____

The only quality interaction I can manage now is...

_____

_____

_____

After a treatment, I...

_____

_____

_____

It is normal to feel sad, angry, and distressed about the changes...

_____

_____

_____

When someone asks me how I feel, I...

_____

_____

_____

I feel extremely vulnerable when...

_____

_____

_____

I am jumping to conclusions about...

_____

_____

_____

Will I experience reduced performance?

_____

_____

_____

Will sexual intercourse change because of the treatment?

_____

_____

_____

The concerns I have about sexual intimacy are...

_____

_____

_____

It is important to communicate openly in my sexual relationship by...

_____

_____

_____

Treatment fatigue is...

_____

_____

_____

I fear losing physical control when...

_____

_____

_____

My attention span...

_____

_____

_____

Today I feel...

_____

_____

_____

It is exhausting to think about...

_____

_____

_____

Will a positive attitude help my experience of the treatment?

_____

_____

_____

The first change in my body that I became aware of was...

_____

_____

_____

Cancer has taken over my life because...

_____

_____

_____

It has already been eighty days, and...

_____

_____

_____

Looking back on the past two months, I...

_____

_____

_____

Some days I become automated and...

_____

_____

_____

I struggle to stay mentally fit while my body...

_____

_____

_____

My most severe aftereffects are...

_____

_____

_____

Adhering to my treatment is...

_____

_____

_____

It feels as if my body has failed me when...

_____

_____

_____

Some of my decreased physical skills are...

_____

_____

_____

I feel insecure about physical changes that aren't visible to others, such as...

_____

_____

_____

I have to take time to grieve physical losses and adjust to...

_____

_____

_____

Day 85 of 365

Date:................................

I try to prepare for a treatment by...

_____

_____

_____

When I feel physically weakened, I...

_____

_____

_____

After treatment, I allow myself time to...

_____

_____

_____

Faith is...

_____

_____

_____

Even if my body changes, I am still...

_____

_____

_____

To be alive with this disease means...

_____

_____

_____

The aftereffect I can handle the least is...

_____

_____

_____

Thriving physically means...

_____

_____

_____

Some days I am too tired to...

_____

_____

_____

Being taken care of by others...

_____

_____

_____

Before every treatment, I feel...

_____

_____

_____

Will I still be attractive to those around me?

_____

_____

_____

The three to five days after a treatment, my family...

_____

_____

_____

The three to five days after a treatment, I focus on...

_____

_____

_____

What helps me most to recover is...

_____

_____

_____

Are my treatments what I thought they would be?

_____

_____

_____

My worst thought about a treatment is...

_____

_____

_____

My best thought about a treatment is...

_____

_____

_____

I experience a heightened sense of...

_____

_____

_____

Is the treatment changing my personality?

_____

_____

_____

Is this the most invested I have been in my own
health?

_____

_____

_____

When I experience trouble doing the usual activities of daily living, I...

_____

_____

_____

Has my fear or sadness had a serious effect on my basic functioning?

_____

_____

_____

What significant changes have I made to my life since a treatment?

_____

_____

_____

# DAYS 93–122

# EMOTIONAL PAIN
# AND GUILT

With cancer, there are many unknowns. There is no *right* way to feel. Some people might feel that they have done something wrong to bring this on, but that is simply not true. It is only natural to want to apportion blame; however, adding guilt on top of something that is patently beyond your control will be detrimental to your emotional well-being, and it does not really warrant your constructive time. This, however, does not mean that you won't feel the need to blame; by voicing it, you can begin to understand that cancer happens indiscriminately and surely to nobody by choice. As you write down your feelings, you will come to notice which ones pass with time and which linger longer. This will provide an indication of where your emotional focus should be. Nobody can really know your pain, and nobody can manifestly tell you when and how to deal with it. Therefore, sharing your thoughts and feelings, even only on paper, is as good a place as any to start. Take care of your emotional pain. It will bring some relief.

Date:........................

My life was established, but...

_____

_____

_____

I don't understand the mechanics of cancer completely; therefore...

_____

_____

_____

My main problem-solving strategy is...

_____

_____

_____

Do my caregivers follow a formal support program?

_____

_____

_____

My biggest support comes from...

_____

_____

_____

When I need emotional guidance, I turn to...

_____

_____

_____

I feel the burden of my family's distress when...

_____

_____

_____

How will my family get through the rough times?

_____

_____

_____

My most challenging task now is...

_____

_____

_____

To stay grounded in my reality, I...

_____

_____

_____

A way that I cope with pain and guilt is...

_____

_____

_____

Do I have to restrict my emotions?

_____

_____

_____

When I become distressed, I seek help from...

_____

_____

_____

Shock replaced with suffering of unbelievable emotional pain...

_____

_____

_____

I feel remorse over things I did or didn't do, such as...

_____

_____

_____

It is important to experience pain fully and completely, which means...

_____

_____

_____

How do I not feel responsible for my own fate?

_____

_____

_____

I feel guilty about...

_____

_____

_____

To escape from pain, I...

_____

_____

_____

Life feels so chaotic when...

_____

_____

_____

I look in the mirror, and...

_____

_____

_____

I wholeheartedly want to...

_____

_____

_____

I am waiting for...

_____

_____

_____

Every day now, I tell myself...

_____

_____

_____

I try to hide my pain by...

_____

_____

_____

Crying helps me to...

_____

_____

_____

I try not to get discouraged when...

_____

_____

_____

Is it OK to cry in public?

_____

_____

_____

The things I expect to happen are...

_____

_____

_____

Can I die from this?

_____

_____

_____

The worst possible thing that can happen is...

_____

_____

_____

I blame...

_____

_____

_____

Positive self-talk will...

_____

_____

_____

Do I have to act OK all the time?

_____

_____

_____

At nighttime, I...

_____

_____

_____

Some days, I cannot cope because...

_____

_____

_____

Sharing my pain and feelings can be...

_____

_____

_____

What am I afraid might happen?

_____

_____

_____

On days when I don't want to see anybody, I...

_____

_____

_____

Who am I becoming?

_____

_____

_____

My initial shock has been replaced by...

_____

_____

_____

Do I have to try to regulate my emotions?

_____

_____

_____

Suffering this unbelievable emotional pain is...

_____

_____

_____

I now think of the importance of enjoying...

_____

_____

_____

I understand I have to experience my pain fully, so I...

_____

_____

_____

What do people think when they look at me?

_____

_____

_____

I am holding myself back from...

_____

_____

_____

Have I fully accepted that I have cancer?

_____

_____

_____

Is it not possible to escape this?

_____

_____

_____

I feel guilty about not...

_____

_____

_____

I have to challenge myself deep inside; otherwise...

_____

_____

_____

I feel remorse over...

_____

_____

_____

How do I give meaning to any of this?

_____

_____

_____

Negative self-talk will...

_____

_____

_____

Sometimes it is hard to be hopeful because...

_____

_____

_____

I deeply believe that...

_____

_____

_____

I manage my stress by...

_____

_____

_____

I want to mend...

_____

_____

_____

Could I have prevented my cancer?

_____

_____

_____

The thought of giving in to it all...

_____

_____

_____

Date:............................

My life feels chaotic when...

_____

_____

_____

I feel trapped when...

_____

_____

_____

Will I ever feel light again?

_____

_____

_____

Day 114 of 365 Date:...........................

Laughter does not come easy anymore...

_____

_____

_____

The days I am happy, I feel guilty because...

_____

_____

_____

The days I am sad, I feel guilty because...

_____

_____

_____

134

Hope is in short supply when...

---

---

---

Some days, my emotions feel out of control...

---

---

---

My high emotional moments are...

---

---

---

I tell my family that...

_____

_____

_____

I express my sadness through...

_____

_____

_____

At unexpected moments, I...

_____

_____

_____

I know the times when I tend to be sad, so I...

_____

_____

_____

I am not to blame for...

_____

_____

_____

Crying for long periods of time...

_____

_____

_____

I have conflicting thoughts about...

_____

_____

_____

My high emotional moments are limited when...

_____

_____

_____

I have to try to see cancer as a mere obstacle in my path, so I must...

_____

_____

_____

I have lost interest in...

_____

_____

_____

My heart aches for...

_____

_____

_____

It is hard to manage my relationships because...

_____

_____

_____

I fear social withdrawal, especially...

_____

_____

_____

Is the emotional effect of cancer more stressful than the physical?

_____

_____

_____

Intrusive thoughts I have are...

_____

_____

_____

Becoming emotionally immersed in cancer feels...

_____

_____

_____

I fear emotional paralysis when...

_____

_____

_____

Looking back on the past months, I...

_____

_____

_____

What message is cancer giving me?

_____

_____

_____

I want to predict my every emotion because...

_____

_____

_____

How do I get to a stronger emotional level?

_____

_____

_____

# DAYS 123–152

# ANGER AND BARGAINING

**B**eing angry might be an indication that you are starting to accept your cancer, and as time passes, you may start to identify patterns in your feelings. Some feelings of anger will still surface from time to time. You are, of course, entitled to be angry about your illness, as it is only natural to feel angry, frightened, stressed, and generally unwell as a result. You need to let people close to you know that your anger is directed at the illness and not at them.

Bargaining results from you attempting to make sense of why the cancer happened to you or because you are trying to prevent future issues from happening to you. Bargaining usually presents in the form of "if only…" statements. It can take the form of promises about lifestyle changes, the offering of something in return for good health, or the like. Bargaining is a natural phase that anyone experiencing trauma in one shape or another undergoes. One cannot turn back time; however, knowing what it is that you feel will contribute to you experiencing your overall cancer ordeal in a less threatening way.

Sometimes I feel abandoned...

_____

_____

_____

I am angry about...

_____

_____

_____

These first few months have been...

_____

_____

_____

I don't want to think about...

_____

_____

_____

I have difficulty concentrating on...

_____

_____

_____

What have I done to...

_____

_____

_____

My frustration makes me so angry that...

_____

_____

_____

Expressing my anger helps me to...

_____

_____

_____

Where can I be safe?

_____

_____

_____

Day 126 of 365

I want to lash out at...

_____

_____

_____

All the stories about cancer make me...

_____

_____

_____

How can I trust my own body again?

_____

_____

_____

I lay unwarranted blame on...

_____

_____

_____

I want to avoid anything related to cancer, including...

_____

_____

_____

My emotions are bottled up, which feels...

_____

_____

_____

Cancer has given me a new title...

_____

_____

_____

Outbursts of anger are...

_____

_____

_____

I try to bargain with powers around me by...

_____

_____

_____

I am angry at my own lost emotions, especially...

_____

_____

_____

If I could trade something, I would...

_____

_____

_____

Is there a way out of this despair?

_____

_____

_____

Sometimes my temper flares up, and I...

_____

_____

_____

I am sorry about...

_____

_____

_____

When people give me reassuring advice, I...

_____

_____

_____

How do I let a bit of laughter in?

_____

_____

_____

When I am cancer-free, I will...

_____

_____

_____

If only I could change...

_____

_____

_____

I cannot stop thinking about...

_____

_____

_____


Will things ever be good again?

_____

_____

_____


My cancer's impact on others is...

_____

_____

_____

My most negative thought right now is...

_____

_____

_____

Sacrifice is...

_____

_____

_____

I have to try to keep the anger out because...

_____

_____

_____

Expressing my anger to others...

_____

_____

_____

My mind tells me...

_____

_____

_____

Am I now solely being defined by my cancer?

_____

_____

_____

Will I become less angry in time?

_____

_____

_____

I criticize myself for...

_____

_____

_____

How do I not "become" cancer?

_____

_____

_____

What will the next challenge be?

_____

_____

_____

In exchange for my health, I will...

_____

_____

_____

Cancer is an obstacle that...

_____

_____

_____

I desperately want to go back to...

_____

_____

_____

If only I could get my life back, I would...

_____

_____

_____

My cancer caused me to...

_____

_____

_____

What else is in the cards for me?

_____

_____

_____

What does my anger need in order to find peace?

_____

_____

_____

I feel betrayed by...

_____

_____

_____

Nobody understands what...

_____

_____

_____

I feel powerless to...

_____

_____

_____

Focusing on worries will...

_____

_____

_____

I am angry at people for no reason...

_____

_____

_____

My quality of life has...

_____

_____

_____

Cancer feels like a dark cloud over my head when...

_____

_____

_____

Can I be angry at the world?

_____

_____

_____

Cancer kicked me out of my comfort zone...

_____

_____

_____

I struggle to maintain a positive outlook when...

_____

_____

_____

If I could turn back time, I would...

_____

_____

_____

If I could go away, I would go...

_____

_____

_____

Can I see the end of my cancer?

_____

_____

_____

Do I wear a mask in front of others?

_____

_____

_____

Do I become discouraged with this whole encounter?

_____

_____

_____

When the going gets tough, I...

_____

_____

_____

I became insecure because...

_____

_____

_____

All the questions I ask myself...

_____

_____

_____

I feel aggressive when...

_____

_____

_____

Cancer has affected my social life in many ways...

It is hard to develop trust in...

How will I keep going?

All my feelings seem so intense, especially...

_____

_____

_____

My emotions change daily and even hourly...

_____

_____

_____

It is not wise to compare myself with others
because...

_____

_____

_____

I became frustrated with the whole medical procedure when...

_____

_____

_____

Do my feelings of anger mean I have fully accepted my cancer?

_____

_____

_____

My life cannot be bargained for, which means that...

_____

_____

_____

Some days, my anger motivates me to take action, such as...

_____

_____

_____

My chance of living beyond cancer is...

_____

_____

_____

I can't seem to relax for long periods of time, especially when...

_____

_____

_____

Is it OK to share my anger with family and friends?

_____

_____

_____

I have to get over this anger to help my body heal better, so I need to...

_____

_____

_____

What will my anger contribute to my life?

_____

_____

_____

I don't want to harbor negative feelings anymore, so I have to...

_____

_____

_____

I have to let go of...

_____

_____

_____

My cancer is what it is, so I have to...

_____

_____

_____

Redirecting anger constructively can help me to...

_____

_____

_____

Consciously choosing to be more peaceful will...

_____

_____

_____

To release all negative feelings would...

_____

_____

_____

Owning my choice to be calm and peaceful helps to...

_____

_____

_____

I will replace feelings of anger with...

_____

_____

_____

Tomorrow will bring...

_____

_____

_____

# DAYS 153—183

# LIFE AROUND ME

*L*ife goes on, and even in this distressing situation, you can definitely take part in that life. Thinking about joy and meaning will help you define yourself in the future even if things may look bleak at the moment. Cancer has brought the opportunity to find new interests, to meet new people, and to gain new insights and meanings. It provides you with *do-over* choices without hesitation; you can set new boundaries and walk through open doors or close some. You can choose otherwise from now on, and if you don't want to, that is also OK. Life does, however, keep on happening, and joining in again at your own time and pace is an exciting and generally uplifting prospect. Living through pain is an enormous accomplishment, and you have every right to keep on living at full force.

Is my cancer giving me a new voice?

_____

_____

_____

I believe in...

_____

_____

_____

Life does not guarantee...

_____

_____

_____

Humor and laughter...

_____

_____

_____

I am thankful for...

_____

_____

_____

Looking back on the past five months, I...

_____

_____

_____

To me, true happiness means...

_____

_____

_____

Today I laughed about...

_____

_____

_____

Now is a time to reflect on my spiritual beliefs because...

_____

_____

_____

I am still part of life around me and...

_____

_____

_____

Spending time in nature will help to...

_____

_____

_____

Where will I fit in after cancer?

_____

_____

_____

Cancer has changed me forever because...

_____

_____

_____

The value I place on life has changed...

_____

_____

_____

The buzz of people going about their day can be...

_____

_____

_____

The compassion of people...

_____

_____

_____

Receiving so much love from people around me
feels...

_____

_____

_____

I try to plan my days the way I have always done,
including...

_____

_____

_____

I am too busy with cancer to notice...

_____

_____

_____

My cancer is serious compared to...

_____

_____

_____

Everything I have now has become...

_____

_____

_____

New friendships...

_____

_____

_____

My view of others with illnesses...

_____

_____

_____

When I look at strangers, I think...

_____

_____

_____

To fit into a world that is constantly on the move, I have to...

I try not to limit the things I want to do just because I have cancer, especially...

Expanding any life interest now will...

I am looking for reasons to enjoy life, such as...

_____

_____

_____

Some days, I function happily in my surroundings...

_____

_____

_____

Joyful moments I've had lately include...

_____

_____

_____

Other people make it seem so easy to just live...

_____

_____

_____

I want to actively engage in...

_____

_____

_____

Having a productive life means...

_____

_____

_____

I want to get inspired by...

_____

_____

_____

How can I make a difference?

_____

_____

_____

Remembering that this disease is not a sentence helps me to...

_____

_____

_____

I have to find joy in...

_____

_____

_____

How do I keep up with life?

_____

_____

_____

I try to look for the good in...

_____

_____

_____

Today I did something for...

_____

_____

_____

The sun, which rises every day...

_____

_____

_____

Sometimes my true spirit struggles to surface, especially when...

_____

_____

_____

Will my cancer define me in the future?

_____

_____

_____

How has nature changed for me?

_____

_____

_____

I now see the beauty in...

_____

_____

_____

The sun setting each day...

_____

_____

_____

The smells of life around me...

_____

_____

_____

My new normal consists of...

_____

_____

_____

Today I had fun when...

_____

_____

_____

My boundaries are open to positive people, including...

_____

_____

_____

If I want to think of myself as strong, I have to...

_____

_____

_____

My most positive thought right now is...

_____

_____

_____

Working through this experience means...

_____

_____

_____

Keeping my spirits high involves...

_____

_____

_____

I am still a normal, everyday person in many ways...

_____

_____

_____

The ramifications of cancer are...

_____

_____

_____

The most recent event on my mind is...

_____

_____

_____

Painful feelings sometimes get in the way of life...

_____

_____

_____

I still worry that I am a burden on those around
me, especially...

_____

_____

_____

I sometimes envy people's good health and am
ashamed about it...

_____

_____

_____

Lifestyle choices now are important because...

_____

_____

_____

Connecting with the world means...

_____

_____

_____

Being part of society requires me to...

_____

_____

_____

Sometimes I feel I'm looking at life from the outside in, especially when...

_____

_____

_____

I have to do what is right for me, which means...

_____

_____

_____

The little things in life...

_____

_____

_____

I can find joy in life even with my cancer...

_____

_____

_____

I want to do things that are more special to me, such as...

_____

_____

_____

I want to share life with...

_____

_____

_____

As my time with cancer continues, I communicate...

_____

_____

_____

I want to embrace the things that bring me joy, including...

_____

_____

_____

Expressing feelings makes it easier to let go of...

_____

_____

_____

I try to look for the good even in this bad time by...

_____

_____

_____

I can use my energy to focus on wellness by...

_____

_____

_____

Knowing that cancer can happen to anyone makes me feel...

_____

_____

_____

Sometimes I allow myself to give in to my feelings...

_____

_____

_____

Some activities that help me unwind are...

_____

_____

_____

Having a daily schedule gives me some control...

_____

_____

_____

How do I inspire myself?

_____

_____

_____

I try not to dwell on fearful thoughts by...

_____

_____

_____

And life goes on despite...

_____

_____

_____

I want to improve my quality of life by...

_____

_____

_____

The wonder that life can bring after such an ordeal is...

_____

_____

_____

The next-best situation I can wish for is...

_____

_____

_____

Positive experiences will...

_____

_____

_____

The majority of my thoughts are...

_____

_____

_____

Taking things one day at a time means...

_____

_____

_____

To be a part of life around me means...

_____

_____

_____

Being thankful for something means...

_____

_____

_____

I know I am still strong enough for this challenge because...

_____

_____

_____

Enjoying food, love, friends, and everything be-
comes a priority when...

_____

_____

_____

I don't just want to watch the world go by, so I
have to...

_____

_____

_____

I want to be part of life, which includes...

_____

_____

_____

# DAYS 184-213

# DEPRESSION, REFLECTION, AND LONELINESS

Having to confront what you might have lost will, of course, bring great sadness. You may face a number of difficulties, like sleeplessness, lack of energy, constant sadness, unexpected crying, and more. Although this is relatively normal under the circumstances, it is important to be aware if too many of these reactions continue for an extended period, it may lead to longer-term and more severe depression. If this happens to you, you need to seek professional help. Although many people deal with cancer the world over, they are dealing with it in their way and you in yours. This means that you may often feel lonely and isolated with your cancer. Loneliness may impact negatively on your general well-being, and you already have more than enough to deal with.

Take your quiet alone moments, but try to fill your other moments with people and things that will inspire you. Very often, people need to go back in order to move forward. Taking yourself back to eventful times in your life, good and bad, will show you the road you have come this far on. Sometimes life forces us to stop and take time to reflect; from this reflection, can come constructive, meaningful insights and decisions.

Sometimes I still become anxious...

_____

_____

_____

What is the one thing about cancer I will remember forever?

_____

_____

_____

When I get lonely, who is the first person I call? Why?

_____

_____

_____

The difference between me and other people with cancer is...

_____

_____

_____

When I am happy, who is the first person I call? Why?

_____

_____

_____

Will I ever feel better?

_____

_____

_____

What do I need to motivate me?

My life has mostly been...

Who will I be after cancer?

Where will this road take me?

_____

_____

_____

My most valued memory is...

_____

_____

_____

Can I hold myself responsible for my well-being in the future?

_____

_____

_____

The most wonderful period in my life was...

_____

_____

_____

I want to go back to...

_____

_____

_____

My biggest achievement is...

_____

_____

_____

Eternity is...

_____

_____

_____

Does it bring relief to constantly analyze my situation? Why?

_____

_____

_____

Being alone is different from loneliness...

_____

_____

_____

I think most about...

_____

_____

_____

Looking back on the past six months, I...

_____

_____

_____

The fact that I have come this far means...

_____

_____

_____

I'm the one who has cancer, not...

_____

_____

_____

Will I ever not be scared about my health again?

_____

_____

_____

The thoughts going through my mind every day are...

_____

_____

_____

Memorable moments are...

_____

_____

_____

The person who has encouraged me most through-
out my life is...

_____

_____

_____

When I have a quiet moment, I...

_____

_____

_____

Is it OK to feel depressed sometimes?

_____

_____

_____

Will depression become a serious concern?

_____

_____

_____

To guard against continued feelings of depression, I...

_____

_____

_____

The saddest period in my life was...

_____

_____

_____

Will it take tremendous ability to bounce back from cancer?

_____

_____

_____

Thinking back to the day I was diagnosed, I...

_____

_____

_____

Will it ever be possible to overcome this experience?

_____

_____

_____

If I don't want cancer to ruin the rest of my life,
I need to...

_____

_____

_____

Cancer is just a page in the book of my life, which
means...

_____

_____

_____

It drains me emotionally to hear about...

_____

_____

_____

I want to focus on my own needs for now, especially...

_____

_____

_____

Time has always been a great healer...

_____

_____

_____

I get overwhelmed by periods of sad reflection, especially when...

_____

_____

_____

At crucial times during my illness, I...

_____

_____

_____

Believing in a higher power means...

_____

_____

_____

The biggest heartache I experienced before cancer was...

_____

_____

_____

If I want my life to be as complete an experience as possible, I...

_____

_____

_____

The one thing that I would like to do over is...

_____

_____

_____

Positive thinking means different things to different people...

_____

_____

_____

No one can be positive all the time...

_____

_____

_____

My core quality has always been...

_____

_____

_____

Will my cancer make me more grateful for the good things in my life?

_____

_____

_____

When I feel despair coming, I...

_____

_____

_____

The true magnitude of my cancer diagnosis is...

_____

_____

_____

I remember...

_____

_____

_____

Sometimes a feeling of emptiness...

_____

_____

_____

My low emotional moments are...

_____

_____

_____

I am not a failure if I do not cope well all the time.

I can be proud of myself on my good and bad days.

Cancer does not have to be a lonely experience.

Living with my own vulnerability means...

_____

_____

_____

My life is a roller coaster, and...

_____

_____

_____

The memories of my past...

_____

_____

_____

I feel good when...

_____

_____

_____

I feel lonely when...

_____

_____

_____

Was cancer a wake-up call for me?

_____

_____

_____

I feel distant from others when...

_____

_____

_____

Nothing could have prepared me for cancer, but...

_____

_____

_____

My perspective on my life has always been...

_____

_____

_____

How my family and I relate to cancer is fundamentally different in that...

_____

_____

_____

How will my cancer change my family's perspective in the long run?

_____

_____

_____

They are also going through a process of...

_____

_____

_____

Being in a healthy group of people feels...

_____

_____

_____


Sometimes small, everyday hassles become big obstacles because...

_____

_____

_____


I feel estranged from...

_____

_____

_____

Which moments occur more for me, high or low moments?

_____

_____

_____

Cancer has so many sensitivities and sensibilities...

_____

_____

_____

Cancer is a passionate and compassionate issue, which means...

_____

_____

_____

Living with cancer means...

_____

_____

_____

What measures can I put in place to measure my
mental health?

_____

_____

_____

Have I learned how to better manage obstacles in
my life?

_____

_____

_____

Cancer is a disease worthy of all my efforts...

_____

_____

_____

My cancer so far has had an impact on my ability
to...

_____

_____

_____

I will work hard to achieve balance by...

_____

_____

_____

How will I transition to a normal life again?

_____

_____

_____

How do I uplift myself from this point on?

_____

_____

_____

To maintain a sense of coherence through it all, I...

_____

_____

_____

I will find happy thoughts to help me...

_____

_____

_____

When I reflect on the quality of my life, I...

_____

_____

_____

I still feel vulnerable when...

_____

_____

_____

Changes in my life will have to include...

_____

_____

_____

Emotional time-outs can be helpful because...

_____

_____

_____

Coping skills include...

_____

_____

_____

DAYS 214-243

REVISITING FEELINGS

$T$hink back and remember. Write it down. Even if some memories appear not so positive, the process serves to at least enable you to look at those memories from a new perspective, which in turn may provide new insight and closure. The good, wonderful memories will bring a warm glow and serve to lighten your mood. Go back to the beginning or the middle or to your cancer or just now (use your diary). It will help to rethink and to know; it should give you a sense of belonging and of being part of society and life. This is good for the soul. Undealt-with issues should come to the fore, and you can now use the opportunity to deal with and manage those in a way you deem appropriate. You should be able now to choose which of the feelings to hold on to and which ones to let go. You are progressing along your path, and that is a good thing.

My thoughts on spirituality are...

_____

_____

_____

It is easy to be hopeful because...

_____

_____

_____

I have never felt that I...

_____

_____

_____

My parents...

_____

_____

_____

My mother always...

_____

_____

_____

My father always...

_____

_____

_____

My childhood was...

_____

_____

_____

My mother never...

_____

_____

_____

My father never...

_____

_____

_____

The relationship between my parents...

_____

_____

_____

My relationship with my parents...

_____

_____

_____

The house I grew up in...

_____

_____

_____

My childhood house brings to mind...

_____

_____

_____

Memorable childhood moments are...

_____

_____

_____

As a child, I surrounded myself with...

_____

_____

_____

The world I grew up in was...

_____

_____

_____

When I got hurt as a child, I...

_____

_____

_____

My childhood friends were...

_____

_____

_____

The most precious memory of my childhood is...

_____

_____

_____

Looking back on my childhood, I...

_____

_____

_____

If I could change one thing about my childhood, it would be...

_____

_____

_____

Having a loving partner means...

_____

_____

_____

Having a loving family means...

_____

_____

_____

Having loving friends means...

_____

_____

_____

I find comfort in...

_____

_____

_____

I have the desire to...

_____

_____

_____

It can be hard to show my true feelings when...

_____

_____

_____

Looking back on the past seven months, I...

_____

_____

_____

Nonthreatening feelings include...

_____

_____

_____

Threatening feelings I sometimes have are...

_____

_____

_____

I need to embrace...

_____

_____

_____

I feel passionate about...

_____

_____

_____

I am blessed because...

_____

_____

_____

The things I valued most as a child were...

_____

_____

_____

My adult life has been filled with...

_____

_____

_____

Different things have different values now, such as...

_____

_____

_____

The people I cared about most in the past were...

_____

_____

_____

Fostering a positive emotional experience is hard because...

_____

_____

_____

I try to forget the times when...

_____

_____

_____

The people I now care most about...

_____

_____

_____

Fostering a positive emotional experience is easy because...

_____

_____

_____

I think with fondness of the times when...

_____

_____

_____

I get caught up in feelings of...

_____

_____

_____

The most peaceful time in my life was...

_____

_____

_____

My emotions get mixed up between past and present memories...

_____

_____

_____

My perception of good caring has changed to...

_____

_____

_____

Alleviation of physical suffering is...

_____

_____

_____

While I kept up the public show, often I...

_____

_____

_____

I should be thankful for this day, this body, and this life because...

However, I sometimes just feel the reminders of what I've lost, especially...

There is tension between my distance from and closeness to cancer...

Sometimes I pretend to...

_____

_____

_____

Do I communicate my feelings enough?

_____

_____

_____

I try not to reveal my true feelings because...

_____

_____

_____

My feelings and responses to cancer are my data for reflection...

_____

_____

_____

My roller-coaster feelings are confusing because...

_____

_____

_____

I am scared to engage at a deeper level with others because...

_____

_____

_____

What words of encouragement would I give to others with cancer?

_____

_____

_____

How do I want to be encouraged?

_____

_____

_____

How could someone comfort me?

_____

_____

_____

Some of the unwanted changes that cancer brought to my life are...

_____

_____

_____

Some days, I feel peaceful and balanced...

_____

_____

_____

Other days, I feel stressed and fearful...

_____

_____

_____

The biggest demand that cancer brought was...

_____

_____

_____

I am still figuring out what new beliefs cancer will bring...

_____

_____

_____

Cancer forced me to look more closely at my personal beliefs, especially...

_____

_____

_____

I cannot ignore my concerns in the hope that they will go away, so I have to...

_____

_____

_____

I attempt not to become withdrawn when...

_____

_____

_____

I will not judge my turbulent feelings as right or wrong by...

_____

_____

_____

It helps when I share my grief with...

_____

_____

_____

It helps when I share my hope with...

_____

_____

_____

My feelings need care just as my body needs care,
and this includes...

_____

_____

_____

I cannot always outwardly express my emotions, especially when...

_____

_____

_____

Unless someone has been in my shoes, he or she can't understand...

_____

_____

_____

The intensity of my feelings changes from day to day...

_____

_____

_____

Sometimes I have trouble focusing on the future, especially...

_____

_____

_____

Strong emotions and reactions occur when I least expect them...

_____

_____

_____

Sometimes worrying stops me from feeling the best I can...

_____

_____

_____

Cancer has made me reexamine my life and...

_____

_____

_____

Is this disease my fate?

_____

_____

_____

Will my courage to get on with life prevail?

_____

_____

_____

Will I succeed in keeping my emotions healthy?

_____

_____

_____

Long periods of persistent, unrelenting stress can
cause problems, such as...

_____

_____

_____

Feeling overwhelmed can reduce my overall quality
of life, so I have to...

_____

_____

_____

I have to develop common short-term goals with
my family, such as...

_____

_____

_____

We must have a shared view of how to take care
of me, including...

_____

_____

_____

A consolidated-care approach will be to the benefit
of us all because...

_____

_____

_____

Cancer has strained some of my relationships...

_____

_____

_____

Cancer has deepened some of my relationships...

_____

_____

_____

Cancer is not me. I am...

_____

_____

_____

# DAYS 244-273

# THE TURN UPWARD

Adjusting to life while living through a trauma requires courage and determination. Decide what your limits are at any time, and move forward accordingly. Create your own rhythm, and get some routine back. What you've learned about yourself and others up to now is extremely valuable as a point of departure for your future choices. Although the future might be uncertain and comes with some fear, new meanings will guide you as you turn the corner. It does not mean you have to be happy and positive all the time, but taking control of the things you can will be a step toward building your confidence and regaining some security. Getting back to some of the things you enjoyed before cancer will also give you renewed appreciation of them. The new future might be a confusing place at times, as cancer will have changed your frame of reference forever. How you manage the turn upward is entirely up to you.

Adjusting to life with cancer means...

_____

_____

_____

Will cancer happen to me again?

_____

_____

_____

Peace of mind is...

_____

_____

_____

Is my life becoming calmer?

_____

_____

_____

Putting cancer into perspective means...

_____

_____

_____

Is my life getting a rhythm back?

_____

_____

_____

I enjoy having upbeat people around me, especially...

_____

_____

_____

What I like about my life now is...

_____

_____

_____

To positively live and breathe cancer for a time means...

_____

_____

_____

How can I tap into my resilience?

_____

_____

_____

One new insight that cancer has given me is...

_____

_____

_____

To build positive emotional experiences through my cancer, I have to...

_____

_____

_____

I want to cope in a stronger, wiser, and more real-istic way, which means...

It is important to connect with my own power because...

I have already survived for 248 days, and I feel...

I try to lighten up and see the humor in a tough situation by...

_____

_____

_____

It feels extremely good to...

_____

_____

_____

The first thing I will do after cancer is...

_____

_____

_____

I read stories about...

_____

_____

_____

I found new meaning in...

_____

_____

_____

I enjoy recording my own feelings because...

_____

_____

_____

I want to do something enjoyable just for me once
a day, such as...

_____

_____

_____

My life is overflowing with good things too...

_____

_____

_____

I get energized by...

_____

_____

_____

My emotional setbacks are less frequent...

_____

_____

_____

Looking back on the past eight months, I...

_____

_____

_____

I try not to be cancer all the time...

_____

_____

_____

I want to make a difference in...

_____

_____

_____

I get daily guidance from...

_____

_____

_____

I dream about...

_____

_____

_____

An important part of healing is establishing the support I need, including...

_____

_____

_____

How do I prepare for my life as a cancer survivor?

_____

_____

_____

It will be scary to leave the cocoon of my health-care providers, especially...

_____

_____

_____

Knowing that my mind might take longer to heal than my body, I...

_____

_____

_____

The steps I can take to understand feelings I still harbor are...

_____

_____

_____

Some fears will fade but will never go away completely, including...

_____

_____

_____

I am surprised by my inner strengths, such as...

_____

_____

_____

I have to be aware of events that can trigger fears, such as...

_____

_____

_____

I must try to cope with fear by being honest with myself about...

_____

_____

_____

To lead a fulfilled life, I have to...

_____

_____

_____

Getting back to a normal life means I have to...

_____

_____

_____

I can affirm my dreams for the future by...

_____

_____

_____

The qualities required to emotionally survive are...

_____

_____

_____

I have to learn to be proud of my body again by...

_____

_____

_____

Putting my mind at ease will give me a greater sense of...

_____

_____

_____

Renewing my connection with people requires...

_____

_____

_____

Maintaining old and new relationships is...

_____

_____

_____

Projects that I want to start or return to are...

_____

_____

_____

I am excited to explore intimacy again, especially...

_____

_____

_____

Taking intimacy to the next healthy level is...

_____

_____

_____

I have learned a lot about my own sexuality, such as...

_____

_____

_____

Knowing that I don't have to do everything at once feels...

_____

_____

_____

I want to protect my time with positive encounters, such as...

_____

_____

_____

Looking ahead makes me feel vulnerable because...

_____

_____

_____

What helps me to move forward is...

_____

_____

_____

Everything else in my life might compete for attention now, especially...

_____

_____

_____

I must take time to establish a new routine, including...

_____

_____

_____

Lingering feelings of sadness and anger will dissi-
pate when...

_____

_____

_____


I am learning to focus on the ways cancer has
made me stronger, such as...

_____

_____

_____


I am more than the scars that cancer has left
behind; I am...

_____

_____

_____

Date:............................

I am amazed at my own ability to overcome this, especially...

_____

_____

_____

Having a clear vision of the future will...

_____

_____

_____

Being acutely aware of time means...

_____

_____

_____

I am now in a place where I can draw strength from...

_____

_____

_____

A happy medium to make me feel good is...

_____

_____

_____

I can attribute the fact that I have survived this far to...

_____

_____

_____

To accept is to come to terms with...

---

---

---

With acceptance come opportunities for true growth, such as...

---

---

---

I will look with a new perspective on...

---

---

---

Channeling positive energy means...

_____

_____

_____

New rewarding habits I want to acquire are...

_____

_____

_____

Being inwardly strong means...

_____

_____

_____

A new course of direction is opening up, and...

_____

_____

_____

Some days are better than others...

_____

_____

_____

A shift in mind-set that can help me to focus is...

_____

_____

_____

A happy place in my mind is...

_____

_____

_____

Thinking about reconstructing my life again is...

_____

_____

_____

Paving the way for better things involves...

_____

_____

_____

Focusing on surviving cancer constructively means...

_____

_____

_____

If I look from the outside in on my life, I...

_____

_____

_____

Positive conditioning will help to...

_____

_____

_____

I am in a good place to...

_____

_____

_____

Where did I get the strength to come this far?

_____

_____

_____

Reclaiming my identity will...

_____

_____

_____

Managing difficult situations in the future will now...

_____

_____

_____

I will take direction from...

_____

_____

_____

I will draw motivation from...

_____

_____

_____

Peaceful acceptance and moving forward require...

_____

_____

_____

Situations beyond my control require...

_____

_____

_____

I understand that getting healthy again means...

_____

_____

_____

# DAYS 274-303

# ACCEPTANCE AND HOPE

Accepting that you are going through cancer does not mean you have to let go of all your sadness and grief. Acceptance is a very positive indicator that allows you to move on to next and new experiences. It demonstrates that you have shifted the focus from what you have lost through cancer to the reality of your life ahead. Peace and understanding will come with new expectations, which might not always be easy to deal with, but again, the opportunity is there for you to have such. Surely, after cancer, you will want and need more - if not right now, then in the future for sure.

Always having hope is hard work. Staying upbeat and unburdening yourself from the negativity of cancer takes a huge effort. However, hope is an awesome feeling of good things to come; hope keeps us going when the going gets tough. You have been very tough this far, and you are surely qualified to move on to the next chapter of your life.

I am learning to accept that...

_____

_____

_____

I am a person with cancer now, which means...

_____

_____

_____

I believe I will...

_____

_____

_____

I hope for...

_____

_____

_____

I trust in...

_____

_____

_____

Dealing with reality is...

_____

_____

_____

I am still troubled, but...

_____

_____

_____

I exist within this trauma by...

_____

_____

_____

A plan for the future is...

_____

_____

_____

I can think about cancer without intense...

_____

_____

_____

I anticipate better times to come...

_____

_____

_____

Finding joy in the experience of living means...

_____

_____

_____

If I am more comfortable with myself, others will
be too; therefore, I...

_____

_____

_____

I have the courage to...

_____

_____

_____

The most beautiful thing in my life right now is...

_____

_____

_____

Finding a strategy for staying hopeful requires...

_____

_____

_____

It is OK to set small goals for myself and build them up slowly, such as...

_____

_____

_____

I can take each day as it comes and not think ahead too much if I...

_____

_____

_____

Date:...........................

Feeling better happens gradually...

_____

_____

_____

Integrating cancer with my personality means...

_____

_____

_____

Sharing my hope with others feels...

_____

_____

_____

Acceptance brings peace...

_____

_____

_____

Looking back on the past nine months, I...

_____

_____

_____

I will give myself a pat on the back for every task
I manage each day, including...

_____

_____

_____

Acceptance has to be deeply rooted to...

_____

_____

_____

Finding significance in my situation is...

_____

_____

_____

Still being angry at cancer will not bring enlighten-
ment or...

_____

_____

_____

Acceptance does not mean giving up on anything; it means...

_____

_____

_____

At this stage in my cancer process, I know...

_____

_____

_____

I have the desire to become part of...

_____

_____

_____

How do I not turn every ache or pain into cancer in the future?

_____

_____

_____

Settling in after cancer will require...

_____

_____

_____

Becoming a survivor makes me...

_____

_____

_____

I am eager to move on to...

_____

_____

_____

I am eager to feel physically well again, especially...

_____

_____

_____

Some complementary therapies I will consider are...

_____

_____

_____

How will my family adapt to the new me?

_____

_____

_____

I have a new vision for me and my family...

_____

_____

_____

Now I want to take care of others too, especially...

_____

_____

_____

Cancer cannot prescribe all my choices, such as...

_____

_____

_____

What is my new significance?

_____

_____

_____

What value will I add to my daily existence?

_____

_____

_____

How do I stay grounded for myself?

_____

_____

_____

How do I stay grounded for my family?

_____

_____

_____

Should my life be different now?

_____

_____

_____

How will my relationships change with my new awareness?

_____

_____

_____

How will I affect those around me?

_____

_____

_____

What should I include in my new vision for my life?

_____

_____

_____

How do I get to the core of what I want?

_____

_____

_____

How do I get to the core of what I need?

_____

_____

_____

This is no small thing that has happened to me...

_____

_____

_____

Writing down my hopes will help me understand...

_____

_____

_____

Acceptance doesn't mean being cheerful and opti-
mistic all the time...

_____

_____

_____

I will reflect on my courage to face up to an uncertain future by...

_____

_____

_____

Do I now have some control over my body? How or why?

_____

_____

_____

Do I now have some control over my thoughts? How or why?

_____

_____

_____

In my quiet moments, I will stick to what I know and not let my imagination run wild...

_____

_____

_____

What if what I want now is not the same as what my family wants?

_____

_____

_____

Will my family and I grow together from this point on?

_____

_____

_____

Will my family always worry about me in the future?

_____

_____

_____

I don't always have to stop myself from feeling down...

_____

_____

_____

If I need to cry, it is fine to do just that...

_____

_____

_____

If I feel upset, I will find a safe way to express it, such as...

_____

_____

_____

I see my days spent with...

_____

_____

_____

I will constructively pursue...

_____

_____

_____

It is with new dedication that I...

_____

_____

_____

Emotional well-being will be a priority because...

_____

_____

_____

A quest to find my true spirit again will require...

_____

_____

_____

Spiritual awareness is...

_____

_____

_____

My personal journey will become...

_____

_____

_____

My journey through cancer has...

_____

_____

_____

I've come to an understanding of...

_____

_____

_____

Day 298 of 365

Date:...........................

The gift of life is...

_____

_____

_____

I have new appreciation for...

_____

_____

_____

How can I give back to life?

_____

_____

_____

The people who have supported me through this are...

_____

_____

_____

I want to be a testament to the commitment of all my carers by...

_____

_____

_____

People care more than we think...

_____

_____

_____

Some of my behaviors that have changed are...

_____

_____

_____

Some of my behaviors that have not changed are...

_____

_____

_____

Mere existence is not enough anymore...

_____

_____

_____

The one thing that I will set out to accomplish is...

_____

_____

_____

Seeking the value of my own self will be...

_____

_____

_____

Seeking truth in the real world is a challenge that I...

_____

_____

_____

I can put cancer behind me at my own pace if I...

_____

_____

_____

Continued introspection will help me to...

_____

_____

_____

If I could get a glimpse of the future, I would like to see...

_____

_____

_____

Another day, another opportunity to...

_____

_____

_____

Gracefully looking back on the past months, I can now...

_____

_____

_____

Moving forward is a big step toward...

_____

_____

_____

# DAYS 304-334

# RECONSTRUCTING MY LIFE

Your life has been interrupted by cancer, and this unfortunate turn of events very often means that certain changes will be required in different areas of your life, as you will look at people and events differently. Your plan for your career, relationships, parenthood, and retirement will look different. The things you do for fun, the places you travel to, the food you enjoy, and the books you read will require new consideration. It might seem daunting but also exciting. Surviving cancer will most certainly deepen the quality of people and things you surround yourself with. You will certainly look at everything from a new perspective, and this will take practice. As you walk away from your life as you knew it before cancer, you will reignite your sense of vitality. How wonderful can this be?

My coping mechanisms must be healthy and helpful, such as...

_____

_____

_____

I want to focus on new relaxation techniques, such as...

_____

_____

_____

I am becoming more functional...

_____

_____

_____

My mind is working properly again, and...

_____

_____

_____

I am seeking realistic solutions for...

_____

_____

_____

Reconstructing myself means...

_____

_____

_____

Making practical choices requires...

_____

_____

_____

I am positive about...

_____

_____

_____

My five inner strengths are...

_____

_____

_____

I would like to rediscover...

_____

_____

_____

I have new interest in...

_____

_____

_____

I want to renew my...

_____

_____

_____

What's next?

_____

_____

_____

Recovery from cancer means...

_____

_____

_____

The plan for my life is...

_____

_____

_____

How can I reignite a sense of vitality?

_____

_____

_____

What are the three big things I still want to do in life?

_____

_____

_____

Living life more fully means...

_____

_____

_____

How do I constructively place the trauma of cancer in the past?

_____

_____

_____

Have I grown emotionally?

_____

_____

_____

Looking back on the past ten months, I...

_____

_____

_____

I realize now that the foundation of my life is...

_____

_____

_____

The cornerstones to putting my life back together are...

_____

_____

_____

The new building blocks for my life will be...

_____

_____

_____

Walking away from my life as I know it feels...

_____

_____

_____

I don't have to reconstruct my life to what it was prior to cancer...

_____

_____

_____

The future is an exciting place to...

_____

_____

_____

I am not overcome by fear of the future...

_____

_____

_____

Putting the pieces of my life back together is...

_____

_____

_____

Ways that I can ease the transition back to everyday life are...

_____

_____

_____

I will not allow the big C to loom over me by...

_____

_____

_____

I am in the driver's seat...

_____

_____

_____

Change may not take place overnight...

_____

_____

_____

Staying positive takes practice and...

_____

_____

_____

From now on, I will set the tone for...

_____

_____

_____

My life is supported by...

_____

_____

_____

I choose to put my life together by...

_____

_____

_____

Even on sad days, I can be great...

_____

_____

_____

For me now, a symbol of health and strength is...

_____

_____

_____

I will not be crushed under the weight of cancer if I...

_____

_____

_____

I have the freedom to...

_____

_____

_____

Now is the time to be practical about...

_____

_____

_____

I have to accept that there will be some dark days...

_____

_____

_____

Reflecting on my journey over the past ten months, I...

_____

_____

_____

I want to clean my mind to make room for...

_____

_____

_____

Aftercare for mind and body is equally important because...

_____

_____

_____

As time goes by, I will think about my cancer less...

_____

_____

_____

I will find the good even in my bad moments by...

_____

_____

_____

Cancer does not dominate my daily life...

_____

_____

_____

Productive activities are...

_____

_____

_____

I can take quiet moments to...

_____

_____

_____

I revitalize myself by...

_____

_____

_____

Things that will always be symbolic of my cancer are...

_____

_____

_____

Letting go will bring relief and...

_____

_____

_____

It is OK to take time away from...

_____

_____

_____

How was my life before cancer different?

_____

_____

_____

Do I have to live my life as I did before?

_____

_____

_____

What will help me to pass time instead of worrying?

_____

_____

_____

Reminiscing helps to...

_____

_____

_____

A life enhancer for me would be...

_____

_____

_____

Self-help aids that I might use in the future are...

_____

_____

_____

Directing my energy toward complete healing means...

_____

_____

_____

Positive reinforcement means...

_____

_____

_____

To get on with my life, I need to...

_____

_____

_____

How will I overcome some of my obstacles?

_____

_____

_____

The message I would like to convey to others is...

_____

_____

_____

My follow-up care program includes...

_____

_____

_____

My emotional care program includes...

_____

_____

_____

I will focus on what I can control, including...

_____

_____

_____

Today I am thankful for...

_____

_____

_____

I feel relieved to have...

_____

_____

_____

Putting my life in some sort of order will help to...

_____

_____

_____

I have an unexpected mix of emotions about what is to come...

_____

_____

_____

Sometimes I still feel vulnerable and uncertain about the future...

_____

_____

_____

I don't always have a clear picture in my mind of...

_____

_____

_____

The triggers that intensify my worries about cancer are...

_____

_____

_____

I will respond to those triggers by...

_____

_____

_____

I will handle the anxiety surrounding follow-ups by...

_____

_____

_____

I understand that I will have ongoing concerns, such as...

_____

_____

_____

I will welcome continued support and encouragement from...

_____

_____

_____

To adjust to life beyond active treatment means...

_____

_____

_____

My surveillance plan for cancer recurrence is...

_____

_____

_____

A way I will manage the fear of recurrence is...

_____

_____

_____

A survivorship care program is...

_____

_____

_____

I find it comforting and validating to...

_____

_____

_____

My focus on wellness is...

_____

_____

_____

I will not allow destructive thought patterns to...

_____

_____

_____

When I have negative and disruptive thoughts, I...

_____

_____

_____

I will replace unhealthy beliefs and behaviors with...

_____

_____

_____

I will be patient with myself by...

_____

_____

_____

The emotional attributes that led me to where I am today are...

_____

_____

_____

Coping with cancer has made me stronger, wiser, and...

_____

_____

_____

I recognize that I have to delve deep in order to...

_____

_____

_____

DAYS 335–365

THE CHALLENGE

Surviving cancer has its own issues. Once the primary issues are over, you will have to think of what to do next—what to do with your time and how to direct your newfound awareness. By now, you have most probably overcome one of the bigger challenges you have ever faced, and the fact that you are moving forward is rewarding. As you put the pieces of your life back together, you will come to a clear understanding that you are worthy no matter what. You will regain new confidence in your own abilities and draw from the courage you have shown over the past year to choose to live a more extraordinary life from here on. Allowing yourself to be happy after it all will be a huge step toward finding your purpose, to finding other meaning, and on redirecting your energy. You have come a long way, and your survival is good reason to celebrate your spectacular life ahead.

What now?

_____

_____

_____

This is day 335, and I...

_____

_____

_____

The longing to live and laugh from the heart is...

_____

_____

_____

Happiness is the purpose of life...

_____

_____

_____

My happiness depends on my...

_____

_____

_____

Allowing myself to be happy means...

_____

_____

_____

Peace comes at a price...

_____

_____

_____

The choice to have peace after cancer is...

_____

_____

_____

Seeking out the best situation for my life involves...

_____

_____

_____

Not settling for an ordinary life again means...

_____

_____

_____

Breaking out of limiting patterns requires...

_____

_____

_____

Finding true contentment requires...

_____

_____

_____

I have the courage to live a life true to myself,
which means...

_____

_____

_____

I have the courage to express my inner emotions,
such as...

_____

_____

_____

Living the life I want now means...

_____

_____

_____

I am looking at life in new ways...

_____

_____

_____

Staying in touch with new friends means...

_____

_____

_____

Bringing the new me to old acquaintances feels...

_____

_____

_____

I am worthy no matter what happens in my life...

_____

_____

_____

I have regained some confidence in my body...

_____

_____

_____

I will handle whatever comes next by...

_____

_____

_____

Compared to my life before cancer, my life after cancer...

_____

_____

_____

I choose to live a more extraordinary life from now on, which means...

_____

_____

_____

My earthly existence is...

_____

_____

_____

When I reflect on spirituality, purpose, and what I
value most, I...

_____

_____

_____

My expectations for my future are...

_____

_____

_____

The challenges involved in leading as healthy and active a life as possible are...

_____

_____

_____

I have done an end-of-treatment assessment, and...

_____

_____

_____

The full extent of my cancer has presented itself, and...

_____

_____

_____

Cancer has been the beginning of...

_____

_____

_____

My plan for reducing stress includes...

_____

_____

_____

I will relax more by...

_____

_____

_____

Having fun again really is an option...

_____

_____

_____

I will change my life to reflect what matters most now, including...

_____

_____

_____

Issues that might resurface now are...

_____

_____

_____

I plan to deal with these issues by...

_____

_____

_____

Facing forward means...

_____

_____

_____

Possible creative outlets I want to explore are...

_____

_____

_____

A sense of spirituality can become a source of strength...

_____

_____

_____

Searching for personal meaning is a lifelong quest that involves...

_____

_____

_____

Assessing my life and future requires...

_____

_____

_____

I can choose to make life what I want it to be, and I choose...

_____

_____

_____

Coming to terms with a year of dealing with cancer is...

_____

_____

_____

Reaching out and helping others is...

_____

_____

_____

I want to focus my energy on ways that...

_____

_____

_____

My priorities have changed to...

_____

_____

_____

Effective coping requires me to understand the challenges and...

_____

_____

_____

My focus for coping emotionally will be...

_____

_____

_____

I find support during my transition into survivorship from...

---

---

---

Nothing I experience now should hold me back from enjoying my life...

---

---

---

The challenge to remain productive is...

---

---

---

Any limitations caused by my cancer are...

_____

_____

_____

Adjusting to any losses caused by my cancer requires...

_____

_____

_____

Thinking through solutions for posttreatment issues, I...

_____

_____

_____

Recognizing new possibilities has become important, especially...

The course of action I choose must...

Constructing a weekly or monthly goal plan will...

Communication with health-care providers and family is...

_____

_____

_____

Turning to community resources for survivorship support is...

_____

_____

_____

Other forms of support I might consider are...

_____

_____

_____

Are my current roles in my family or as a friend fulfilling?

_____

_____

_____

My core emotional needs right now are...

_____

_____

_____

Getting to know my own intimate emotions is...

_____

_____

_____

Getting on with life after cancer will not always be easy, especially...

_____

_____

_____

My life will resume despite cancer and beyond cancer and...

_____

_____

_____

Being a survivor means I have won...

_____

_____

_____

Becoming available to my loved ones again means...

_____

_____

_____

Breaking up my future into small, manageable chunks will...

_____

_____

_____

Getting on will take time, patience, and...

_____

_____

_____

Date:...........................

Next year, I must...

_____

_____

_____

Some unique challenges that might arise are...

_____

_____

_____

Being a cancer survivor can be demanding when...

_____

_____

_____

Attempts to overfill my time lead to...

_____

_____

_____

Manageable ways of connecting are...

_____

_____

_____

Taking time to enjoy new shared experiences is...

_____

_____

_____

It has been nearly a year since my diagnosis, and...

_____

_____

_____

Making sense of my experience is challenging...

_____

_____

_____

The best way forward is to focus on...

_____

_____

_____

Examining my long-held views and beliefs, I find...

_____

_____

_____

Communicating openly and freely means...

_____

_____

_____

Transitioning back to normality is exciting and...

_____

_____

_____

Being mindful of the way cancer could affect my relationships means...

_____

_____

_____

Opportunities to reconnect with colleagues and friends include...

_____

_____

_____

The value of old and new relationships...

_____

_____

_____

Transitioning back is about finding out what's normal for me now, which includes...

_____

_____

_____

There is comfort in settling back into a regular routine and lifestyle, especially...

_____

_____

_____

I am excited about my new journey of self-discovery because...

_____

_____

_____

Why am I still here?

_____

_____

_____

What is the ultimate purpose of my life?

_____

_____

_____

How can I find my purpose?

_____

_____

_____

Today I celebrate my survival by...

_____

_____

_____

One year on and I...

_____

_____

_____

I have come a long way...

_____

_____

_____

You are more

than your story.

Made in the USA
San Bernardino, CA
05 June 2018